Gardening For Butterflies.

This booklet is for those gardeners who wish to attract butterflies into their gardens and to induce them to linger as long as possible. The plants most likely to do this are not necessarily expensive or difficult to grow. There is a very wide range of plants that are suitable as nectar sources for butterflies. Some of these plants are given in lists for different types of garden with a few planting arrangements. A butterfly garden is not going to be more arduous to keep tidy and enjoyable. Quite the reverse. After all who is going to search for weeds when it's so much more interesting to watch the constantly changing kaleidescope of colour, provided by some of our most charming insects?

Gardens are playing an increasingly important role in helping British butterflies to survive. As more and more natural habitats are turned into concrete, brick and tarmac deserts, it is that much more difficult for butterflies to find nectar. This is essential as it is their main source of energy, which they require to mate and search for a suitable plant on which to deposit their eggs.

Unfortunately there are many gardens and estates, as well as vast areas of open countryside which, although green and colourful, are still deserts as far as butterflies are concerned. Unless there are flowers which produce nectar or suitable plants, grasses and trees on which they can lay their eggs, there will be nothing to attract or sustain them. This booklet should help you to choose those plants which will be most suitable for your garden. Then all you need is a little luck. If we can provide shelter a   ～ ～ᵃᵃⁿ hope that nature will provide warmth and sunshine.

GW00498542

Basic Requirements

Butterflies are said to be "coldblood(warmth before they can become active. As so..   arch for the warmest, sheltered spot to bask in the sun's rays and then find a nectar source. If they can combine the two so much the better. A cold, windswept, overshadowed garden which faces north and is planted with Rhododendrons, Roses, Lilies and Gladioli is only likely to see the occasional butterfly en route to somewhere warmer, sunnier and with flowers which produce nectar available to butterflies.

Many people are under the mistaken impression that a butterfly garden has to be a wilderness but this is not so. A very successful garden can be produced using plants which are usually classified as formal bedding plants. A small garden is naturally limited in it's choice of plants by it's lack of space.It is better to have the most highly recommended plants in good numbers, grown in a few largish groups rather than trying to grow all the plants mentioned in pennynumbers. Medium sized gardens will have the choice of either formal or informal designs designs as long as the plants are not too large. If in doubt, always choose the smaller variety of a type of plant because they are less likely to need staking and they can be planted closer together. This increases the number of flowers available in a given area. Large gardens can have rockeries, formal and informal flower beds, mixed herbaceous beds and shrubberies if desired. There are good varieties of plants for all types of well laid out gardens.

Having chosen which type of garden you wish to have, it is important to know where the warmest and sunniest places are in spring and autumn. This is where the spring and autumn flowering plants should be grown if they are to benefit the butterflies which hibernate over winter. Do not grow large quantities of spring flowers at the expense of summer and autumn ones because the spring flying butterflies do not usually appear in the same numbers as those which fly in summer and autumn.

During summer months, the sun extends into more parts of a garden and summer flowering plants can be grown in these sun exposed beds. Summer flowering plants can often be planted where spring flowers that have finished have been cleared away. An example of this is a display of wallflowers and forgetmenots that can be completely changed at the beginning of June to make way for a summer flowering display of suitable bedding plants. The flowering period of summer plants can often be extended into the autumn by regularly taking off the dead blooms and some will flower until the frost finally kills them. The flowering period of hardy annuals can be extended by sowing a few seeds at fortnightly intervals throughout April and May.

Choice of Plants

Some of the most successful plants that can be grown easily in an average garden include : Buddleias, Sedum spectabile (Pink – but not the hybrid varieties), Lavender, Aubretia, Alyssum, Candytuft, Double Scabious, Phlox and African Marigolds. Most of these plants are mauve and pink and give a very pleasing effect when grown together. There are several plants,however, in the yellow and orange shades which are also attractive to butterflies. Many people wish to 'mix and match' the colour scheme they have chosen for their gardens. The following suggestions are intended to help that choice . These are by no means complete lists of suitable plants.
(* Especially recommended plants)

	white/pink/blue	yellow/orange/red
Patio and Small Gardens		
Spring	*Aubretia (H.P.)	Wallflowers (H.B.)
	Sweet William (H.B.)	Yellow Alyssum (H.P.)
	Forget-me-nots (H.B.)	Polyanthus (H.P.)
	Violets (H.P.)	Primroses (H.P.)
Summer	Dwarf Phlox (H.H.A.)	*Dahlia Coltness Hybrids (H.H.P.)
	*Dwarf Scabious (H.A.)	*Dwarf Helichrysum (H.H.A.)
	Ageratum (H.H.A.)	Mignonette (H.A.)

	*Candytuft (H.A.)	French Marigold
	White Alyssum (H.A.)	"Naughty Marietta"(H.H.A.)
Autumn	Sedum spectabile (H.P.)	Golden Rod dwarf (H.P.)

Medium Formal Gardens. (All the above plus the following)

Summer	*Verbena (H.H.A.)	African Marigold
	Scabious (H.A.)	"Crackerjack" (H.H.A.)
	Phlox (H.P.)	Helichrysum (H.H.A.)
	Aster amellus (H.P.)	Layia elegans (H.H.A.)
	Erigeron (H.P.)	
	Lobelia (H.H.A.)	
	Dianthus (H.H.A.)	

Medium Informal Gardens. (All the above plus the following)

Spring	Honesty (H.B.)	
	Heliotrope (H.H.A.)	Annual Chrysanthemums (H.A.)
	Valerian (H.P.)	Buddleia weyerana
	Nepeta cataria (H.P.)	* "Sun Gold" (H.Shr.)
	Buddleia nanhoensis	Corn Marigold (H.A.)
	(H.Shr.)	Helenium (H.P.)
	Perennial Cornflower (H.P.)	
	Lavender (H.Shr.)	
	Aster sinensis (H.H.A.)	

Large Formal Gardens. (Any of the plants so far listed for formal gardens.)

Large Informal Gardens.

Spring	Buddleia alternifolia	Buddleia globosa
	(H.Shr.)	(H.Shr.)
	Syringa prestonii (H.Shr.)	
Summer	Wild Cornflower (H.A.)	Inula denticulata (H.P.)
	Hemp agrimony (H.P.)	Sunflower (H.A.)
	Teasel (H.P.)	Tithonia "torch" (H.H.A.)
	Echinops (H.P.)	
	Marjoram (H.P.)	
	Hyssop (H.P.)	
Autumn	Michaelmas Daisies (H.P.)	Golden Rod (H.P.)

Shrub Gardens

	Cornus (H.Shr.)	Ivy (H.Cl.)
	Escallonia langleyensis (H.Shr.)	
	Ceratostigma willmottianum (H.Shr.)	
	Hebe spp (H. and H.H.Shr.)	
	Buddleia davidii (H.Shr.)	
	Holly (H.Shr.)	

Wild Area		
	Bramble	Dandelion
	Thistle	Rockrose
	Bugle	Hawkweed
	Violets	Ragwort

Common Blues (above) Small Coppers (centre right) and Wall Browns are all known to use lavender as a source of nectar.

Blackthorn	Pussy Willow
Alder Buckthorn	Fleabane
Hops	Cowslips
Ladies Smock	Birdsfoot Trefoil
Garlic Mustard	Nettles
Privet	
Ivy	

H.A. Hardy annuals can be sown in open ground in September to flower earlier than spring sown seeds. They can withstand frosts.

H.H.A. Half-hardy annuals cannot survive frost. They should not be bedded out in the garden until all risk of frost has passed.

H.B. Hardy biennials are sown in the late summer and the plants bedded out in autumn ready for late spring flowering. They are frost hardy.

H.P. Hardy perennials survive winter conditions. They often die down to ground level in early winter but new shoots emerge each spring.

H.H.P. Half-hardy perennials cannot withstand frost. They need to have protection from low temperatures to grow from year to year.

H.Shr. Hardy shrubs live for many years but may need special pruning for the best results.

H.H.Shr. Half-hardy shrubs will not normally withstand any degree of frost but this group of plants also includes shrubs which can survive in mild and sheltered places and if given some covering in winter.

H.Cl. Hardy climbers will overwinter sucessfully and new growth appears each year.

The cheapest butterfly garden will be obtained from sowing packets of annual seeds. The ground must be dug and perfectly clear of weeds. When the soil has settled and is suitably dry, it should be raked level and lumps of soil broken down until a fine tilth is produced. Read the instructions on the seed packets and take careful note of the height and width of the mature plants; plan the positions of the varieties accordingly. The areas to be sown can then be marked out using short canes. Sand, dribbled along the line of the sown seeds, shows where not to hoe whilst the seeds are germinating. Label each area clearly before going on to the next variety of seed. An example of an inexpensive annual border for a child to grow and also have plenty of flowers to pick is given in fig 1.

More expensive to buy are half-hardy bedding plants which are on sale at nurseries from about the beginning of May. Do not be tempted to buy them until all risk of frost is over for your area if they have to be planted out immediately after purchase.

Shrubs and trees are the most expensive plants to purchase. If grown in containers they can be planted at any time of the year and are available from many nurseries. A golden rule is always to buy from a nursery north of the garden where they are to be planted. If certain shrubs, such as the Hebes, are not on sale, it is a good indication that the missing shrubs may not be hardy enough for that area.

Providing Shelter

Exposed gardens can be improved by the inclusion of shrubs and trees on the northern boundaries. A hedge is superior to a wall for reducing the damaging effects of strong winds, the shelter "band" being approximately four times the height of the hedge. Privet, Hawthorns, Laurel and Holly, if allowed to grow to flowering height, will not only provide good windbreaks but nectar too.

Ivy can be grown over a wooden fence and will become a hedge in it's own right after the original fence has rotted away: a combination known as a "fedge". Old established Ivy serves a dual purpose in giving shelter for hibernating butterflies amongst it's evergreen leaves in winter, and being a valuable source of nectar during winter months. Brimstone butterflies have been seen during every month of the year and if brought out of hibernation by an unseasonable warm spell, will have to replace the energy used to successfully complete the normal hibernation period.

Conifer hedges are not recommended for any but the very largest gardens and estates, it has been suggested that the resinous smell they exude in warm weather might deter some, if not most, of the common butterflies likely to be seen in gardens.

Butterflies

The butterflies that may be attracted into your garden will depend very much on your geographical location, type of soil and the proximity of heathland, grasslands or broadleaf woodlands. Even in conurbations there are parks, canals, railways and allotments which frequently support populations of butterfly species usually associated with woods and open countryside. Small Tortoiseshell, Painted Lady, Red Admiral, Peacock, Large and Small White feed from a wide range of plants and occur in most parts of the British Isles. Woodland species include White Admiral, Speckled Wood and Ringlet and these are not frequently seen in gardens, whereas the meadow grassland species like the Large and Small Skippers and Common Blue can be found in areas of neglected grass and may appear in nearby gardens.

Any good butterfly field guide will give distribution maps of each species of butterfly and will give an indication of which may visit your garden.

The flowers which appeal to a wide range of butterflies and flower for long periods are:—

Aubretia:— Brimstone, Green-veined White, Large White, Orange Tip, Painted Lady, Red Admiral, Small White, Small Tortoiseshell.

Buddleia:— Brimstone, Green-veined White, Large White, Painted Lady, Red

6

Large Whites and Peacocks seek out nectar on flowers of the Dahlia "Coltness hybrids".

Small Skippers (above) and Small Tortoiseshells (below) on Scabious.

Admiral, Small White, Small Tortoiseshell, Comma, Common Blue, Gatekeeper, Marbled White, Meadow Brown, Peacock, Small Skipper, Wall Brown, Speckled Wood.

Candytuft:– Gatekeeper, Large White, Marbled White, Small Tortoiseshell.

Dahlia Coltness Hybrids:– Brimstone, Large White, Painted Lady, Red Admiral, Small Tortoiseshell, Peacock.

Heliotrope:– Comma, Gatekeeper, Large White, Meadow Brown, Painted Lady, Peacock, Small Tortoiseshell, Small White, Speckled Wood.

Lavender:– Brimstone, Green-veined White, Large White, Painted Lady, Small White, Small Copper, Common Blue, Meadow Brown, Small Skipper, Wall Brown.

Scabious (Annual):– Brimstone, Comma, Painted Lady, Peacock, Small Skipper, Small Tortoiseshell.

This is by no means a complete list of all the flowers that butterflies will visit. It does, however, give most of the best plants that have proved reliably attractive to a wide range of butterflies over the years.

Wild flower seeds are becoming more extensively available at garden centres and nurseries. They tend to be more expensive than the cultivated flower seeds but can be obtained through the post from specialist wild flower seed suppliers (eg. Chilterns & Chambers) at very modest prices.

Encouraging butterflies to multiply and flourish.

Each species of butterfly has to lay it's eggs on, or very near to, a specific larval food plant(s). Each family of butterflies has particular chemical requirements for it's larvae (or caterpillars as they are also known) to develop successfully; the plants with the right chemical blend is searched for by the fertile females.

The plants which caterpillars eat are usually not the plants from which the butterfly obtains nectar. Although obvious, it is as well to point out that although butterflies do not disfigure plants at all, caterpillars most certainly do and can strip leaves and seed pods of various plants.

Suitable plants for butterfly larvae to eat.

Large and Small Whites	Plants in the Cabbage family, Nasturtiums.
Brimstone	Alder Buckthorn and Purging Buckthorn.
Orange Tip	Arabis, Ladies Smock, Honesty
Common Blue	Birdsfoot Trefoil
Skippers	Coarse Grasses (e.g. Cocksfoot, Falsebrome)
Small Tortoiseshell, Red Admiral, Peacock	Nettles
Painted lady	Thistle

The plants listed above are those which can easily be grown in any garden. Some of our British butterflies have only one food plant on which their larvae can feed and that food plant may be threatened by modern farming and forestry methods. Only extremely specialised work on the part of dedicated conservationists can hope to keep these food plants in sufficient quantities for endangered species to survive. The Large Copper is an example of this; attempting to grow Great Water Dock in the wrong environment will not bring this butterfly into the cultivated garden.

The use of sprays to control insects.

Whether or not caterpillars are a nuisance in a garden, without them we do not get any butterflies, and as butterflies are insects, all insecticides will kill them. There is no known insecticide which is safe for them, not even those sold at 'organic' garden centres. Dilute common household detergent is an effective spray against green and blackfly which is apparently harmless to butterflies.

Alternative Methods.

Butterflies need sun, warmth and shelter, as stated before, therefore, Nasturtiums and ornamental cabbages which are part of a flowering scheme, and not grown for caterpillars to eat, should be bedded out in the coolest and shadiest parts of the garden. Nasturtiums will grow in the shade of trees in a north facing border and will self seed each year. Unless the shade temperature is steadily in the 80's it is unlikely that any damage will be done.

Fruit netting over cabbages will not only help to keep butterflies off but also pigeons. The Large and Small White butterflies which do succeed in laying their eggs on the winter greens can be reared by sacrificing one or two plants on which the caterpillars are allowed to feed, removing any found on other plants. A compromise between conserving wildlife and food.

Conclusion

If this booklet has fired your enthusiasm and you decide to turn over at least some, if not all, of your garden for encouraging butterflies, would you consider helping further? The B.B.C.S. has branches in most regions and your sightings are of value to them particularly if sent in regularly each year.

The records to keep are:– Species, date seen, location, approximate numbers.

The name and address of your nearest branch is available from The British Butterfly Conservation Society, Tudor House, Quorn, Nr., Loughborough, Leics, LE12 8AD.

Another positive step is to join the above society if you have not already done so, and thus help to increase the general public's awareness of the all pervading threat to our most beautiful, endangered insects.

Painted Ladies (top left), a Red Admiral (top right), Commas (centre), Gatekeepers (lower left) and a Marbled White (lower right) take nectar from Buddleia davidii blooms.

Brimstone (top), Orange Tips (middle) and Green-veined Whites (below) feeding on Aubretia.

Further Reading

On Butterflies:–

A Complete Guide to British Butterflies – M.Brookes & C.Knight

The Mitchell Beazley Guide to Butterflies – P.Whalley

Collins: The Butterflies of Britain & Europe – L.Higgins & B.Hargreaves

R.S.N.C. Guide to Butterflies of the British Isles – J.A.Thomas

British Butterflies – A Field Guide – R.Goodden

On butterfly gardening and managing wild areas:–

Garden Plants for Butterflies – M.Oates

National Association for Environmental Education Booklet –
Creating and Maintaining a Garden to Attract Butterflies – J.Killingbeck

Amateur Entomologist's Society booklet –
How to Encourage Butterflies to Live in Your Garden – P.W.Cribb

PLANS FOR SMALL GARDENS

HARDY ANNUALS FROM SEED

(white/pink/mauve)

Fig. 1

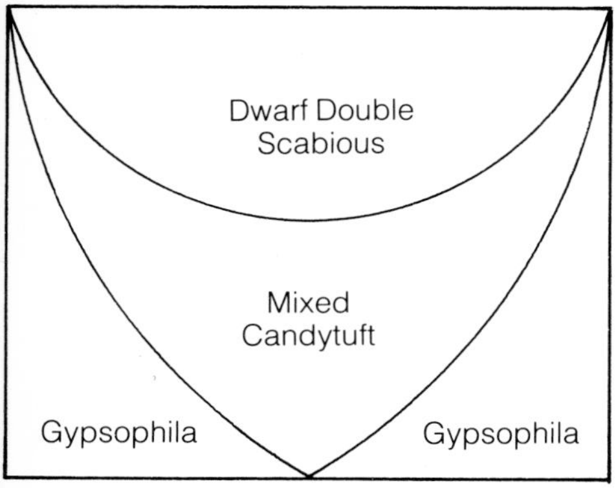

Dwarf Double
Scabious

Mixed
Candytuft

Gypsophila   Gypsophila

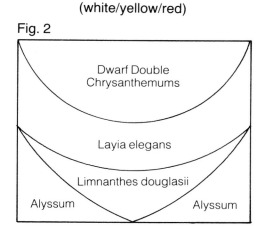

(white/yellow/red)

Fig. 2

Dwarf Double
Chrysanthemums

Layia elegans

Limnanthes douglasii

Alyssum   Alyssum

HALF-HARDY ANNUALS
(Available at Garden Centres)

(white/pink/mauve)

Fig. 3

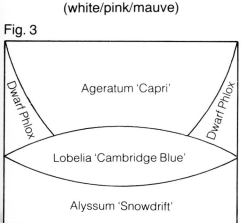

Dwarf Phlox

Ageratum 'Capri'

Dwarf Phlox

Lobelia 'Cambridge Blue'

Alyssum 'Snowdrift'

(white/yellow/red)

Fig. 4

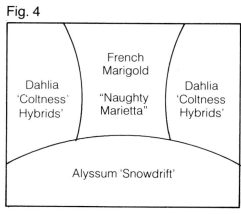

French
Marigold

Dahlia
'Coltness'
Hybrids'

"Naughty
Marietta"

Dahlia
'Coltness'
Hybrids'

Alyssum 'Snowdrift'

HARDY ANNUALS FROM SEED

(white/pink/mauve)

Fig. 5

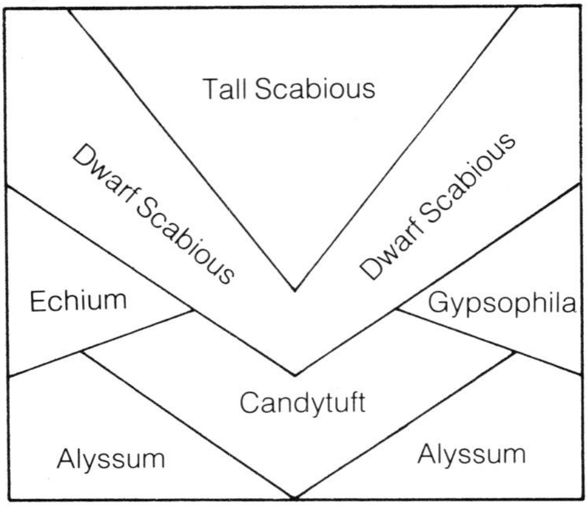

Tall Scabious

Dwarf Scabious

Dwarf Scabious

Echium

Gypsophila

Candytuft

Alyssum

Alyssum

(white/yellow/red)

Fig. 6

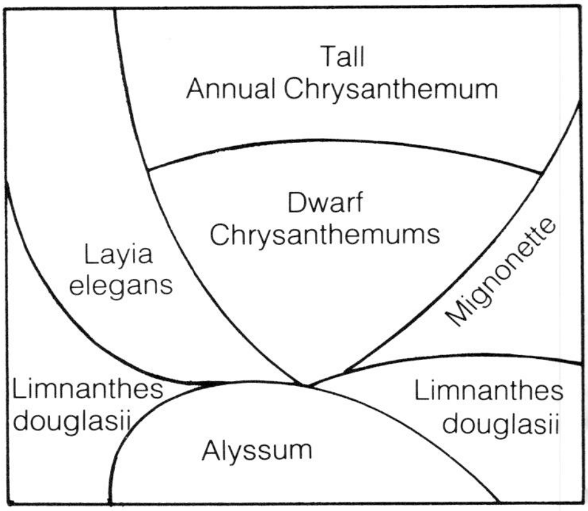

Tall
Annual Chrysanthemum

Dwarf
Chrysanthemums

Layia
elegans

Mignonette

Limnanthes
douglasii

Limnanthes
douglasii

Alyssum

HALF-HARDY PLANTS
(Available at Garden Centres)

(white/pink/mauve)

Fig. 7

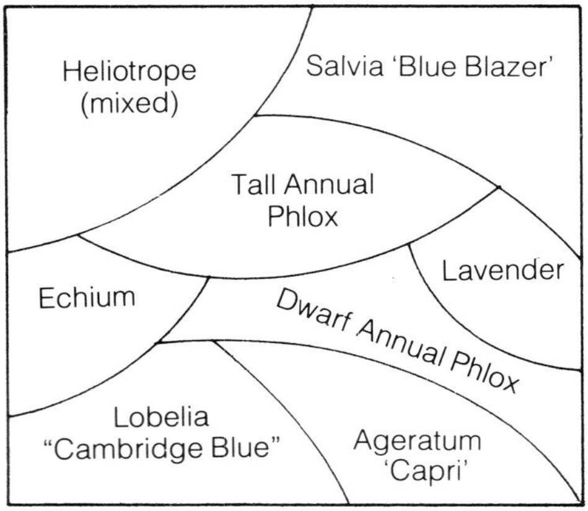

Heliotrope
(mixed)

Salvia 'Blue Blazer'

Tall Annual
Phlox

Lavender

Echium

Dwarf Annual Phlox

Lobelia
"Cambridge Blue"

Ageratum
'Capri'

(white/yellow/red)

Fig. 8

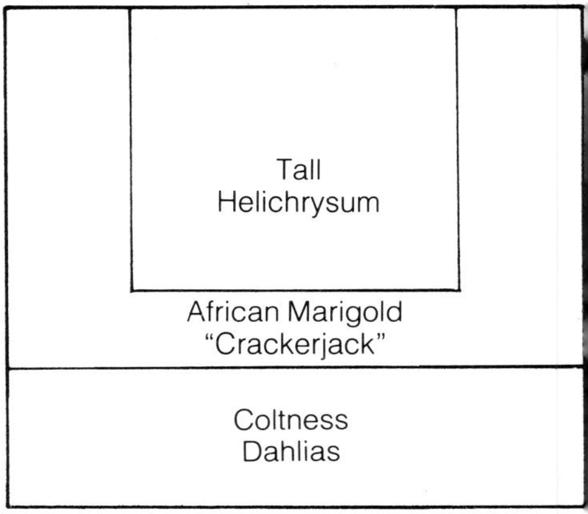

Tall
Helichrysum

African Marigold
"Crackerjack"

Coltness
Dahlias

14

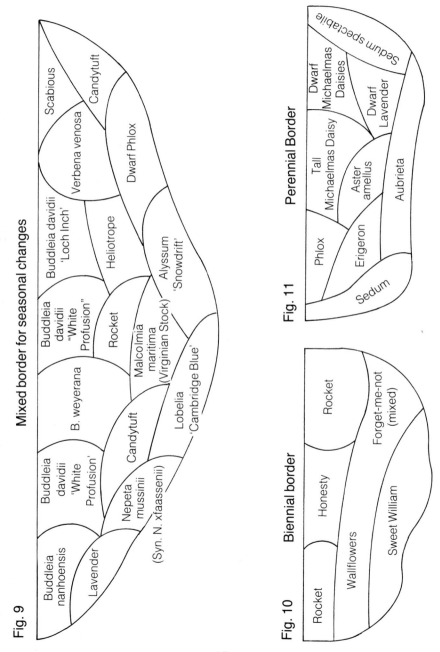

Fig. 9

Mixed border for seasonal changes

Buddleia nanhoensis

Lavender

Buddleia davidii 'White Profusion'

B. weyerana

Nepeta mussinii
(Syn. N. xfaassenii)

Candytuft

Buddleia davidii "White Profusion"

Buddleia davidii "Loch Inch"

Verbena venosa

Scabious

Candytuft

Dwarf Phlox

Heliotrope

Rocket

Malcolmia maritima (Virginian Stock)

Lobelia 'Cambridge Blue'

Alyssum 'Snowdrift'

Fig. 10 Biennial border

Rocket

Honesty

Wallflowers

Rocket

Sweet William

Forget-me-not (mixed)

Fig. 11 Perennial Border

Phlox

Tall Michaelmas Daisy

Aster amellus

Erigeron

Sedum

Dwarf Michaelmas Daisies

Dwarf Lavender

Aubrieta

Sedum spectabile

Fig. 12

Large Garden Corner Shrubbery

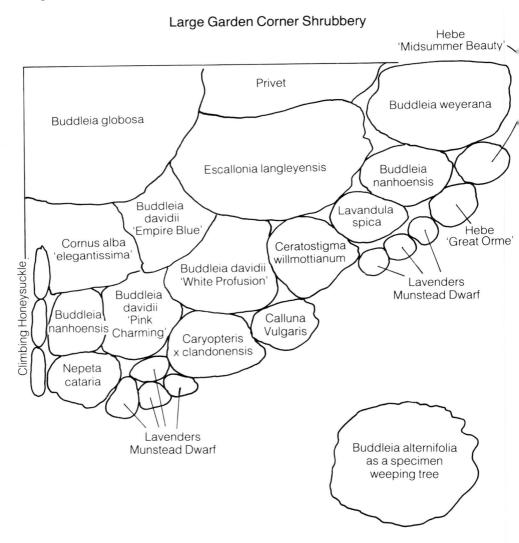

Hebe 'Midsummer Beauty'

Privet

Buddleia weyerana

Buddleia globosa

Escallonia langleyensis

Buddleia nanhoensis

Buddleia davidii 'Empire Blue'

Lavandula spica

Hebe 'Great Orme'

Cornus alba 'elegantissima'

Ceratostigma willmottianum

Climbing Honeysuckle

Buddleia davidii 'White Profusion'

Lavenders Munstead Dwarf

Buddleia davidii 'Pink Charming'

Buddleia nanhoensis

Calluna Vulgaris

Caryopteris x clandonensis

Nepeta cataria

Lavenders Munstead Dwarf

Buddleia alternifolia as a specimen weeping tree

16